# The Gym Teacher
## from the
# Black Lagoon

### by Mike Thaler
### pictures by Jared Lee

SCHOLASTIC INC.
New York   Toronto   London   Auckland   Sydney

For Alan Boyko,
a friend indeed!
— M. T.

To my big brother,
whose first name rhymes with gym.
— J. L.

ISBN 0-590-47917-2

Text copyright © 1994 by Mike Thaler.
Illustrations copyright © 1994 by Jared D. Lee Studio, Inc.
All rights reserved. Published by Scholastic Inc.

We're getting a new gym teacher this year.

He's coming over from the Junior High.
His name is
*Mr. Green*!

The kids say he's big,
he's mean, he's rarely seen.

They say he's *very* hairy,
and his knuckles touch the ground.

His nickname is COACH KONG and no one
has actually heard him speak any words.

He just blows his whistle a lot.

They say he has a little office
full of balls and clubs and tires.

The big kids say he makes you run a lot.
First a lap around the gym.

# Then a lap around the school.

Then a lap around the world!

Then he gives you fitness tests.
You have to lift his pickup truck
over your head before the semester ends.
I guess that's why they call it a "pickup" truck.

You spend a lot of time getting in shape.
He makes you do push-ups, pull-ups,
chin-ups, and sit-ups.
But most of the kids just do *throw-ups*.

Then you have to climb THE ROPE.
If you don't reach the top, he sets the bottom on fire!

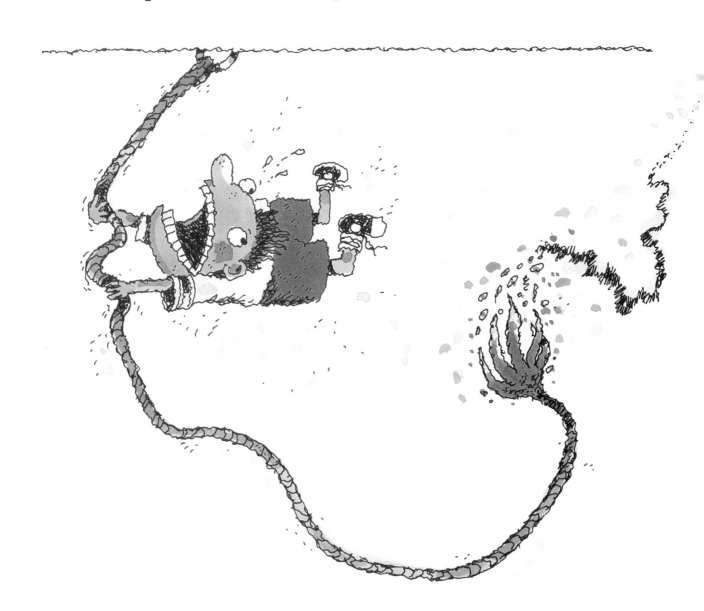

They say there are still kids up in the ceiling
of the Junior High gym.

If you don't pass the fitness tests,
your body is *donated* to science.

Then there's the posture test.
If you don't pass that, he ties you between two boards.

But there are games, too.
He makes you play DODGE ball . . .

with his truck!

And TAG with Crazy Glue . . .

# And baseball with real bats!

Then there's THE PARACHUTE!
He has us all hold on tight to the side
and jump out of an airplane.

He's also big on gymnastics.
He makes you walk "the beam"

and jump over "the horse."

He makes you do

HANDSTANDS,

HEADSTANDS,

NOSE STANDS,

and MUSIC STANDS.

# He makes you do SOMERSAULTS

## and CARTWHEELS.

But the worst thing is SQUARE DANCING . . . with the *girls*!

Oh, oh! There's his whistle!
I better go line up.

"Hi, kids. I'm Mr. Green, your new gym teacher."
I can't believe it!
He's a regular guy!

"Let's play some basketball," says Mr. Green.
We do, and I score two baskets.

This is great!
I'm going to like gym.